Tobacco Use

Perspectives on Physical Health

by Bonnie Graves

Consultant:
Paul Pentel, MD
Department of Medicine
Hennepin County Medical Center
and
University of Minnesota

LifeMatters
an imprint of Capstone Press
Mankato, Minnesota

LifeMatters Books are published by Capstone Press
PO Box 669 • 151 Good Counsel Drive • Mankato, Minnesota 56002
http://www.capstone-press.com

Printed in the United States of America

Library of Congress Cataloging-in-Publication Data
Graves, Bonnie B.
      Tobacco use / by Bonnie Graves.
            p.   cm.—(Perspectives on physical health)
      Includes bibliographical references and index.
      Summary: Discusses the history of tobacco, tobacco addiction, influences on tobacco use, consequences, and suggestions on how to quit or never start using tobacco.
      ISBN 0-7368-0414-5 (book)—ISBN 0-7368-0438-2 (series)
      1. Tobacco habit—Juvenile literature. 2. Smoking—Juvenile literature.
      3. Teenagers—Tobacco use—Juvenile literature. 4. Tobacco habit—Prevention—Juvenile literature. [1. Smoking. 2. Tobacco habit.] I. Title.
      HV5735 .G73 2000
      362.29′6—dc21
                                               99-048087
                                             CIP

Staff Credits
Rebecca Aldridge, editor; Adam Lazar, designer; Mary Donnelly, photo researcher

Photo Credits
Cover: PNI/©StockByte
FPG International/©Elizabeth Simpson, 8; ©Jonathan Meyers, 15; ©Arthur Tilley, 33
International Stock/©Michael Ventura, 30; ©Bill Stanton, 55
©James L. Shaffer/7, 19
©PhotoDisc/Barbara Penoyar, 58
Photo Network/©Eric R. Berndt, 42; ©David N. Davis, 49
Photri, Inc./11; ©Skjold, 56
PNI/©Digital Vision, 16; ©Rubberball, 29; ©StockByte, 46
Uniphoto/©Dennis Johnson, 36; ©Llewellyn, 39; ©Billy E. Barnes, 50
Visuals Unlimited/22; ©Arthur Morris, 40

A 0 9 8 7 6 5 4 3 2 1

Table of Contents

Chapter Overview

Smoking can cause serious health problems. Three million people worldwide die each year from smoking-related illnesses.

Tobacco contains hundreds of different chemicals. Many of these are toxic. When burned, tobacco produces additional deadly compounds such as carbon monoxide and tar.

Secondhand and sidestream smoke can harm nonsmokers.

Cigars and smokeless tobacco can be just as dangerous as cigarettes.

Chapter 1

The Lowdown on Tobacco

Cal sat with Brandon in his car.
They were waiting for Mark to
finish basketball practice. Brandon lit up a cigarette. He took a long drag and blew out the smoke. Cal couldn't help thinking how cool Brandon looked. Cal was a freshman. He looked up to Brandon, who was a junior.

"Hey, look who thinks he's Joe Cool!" Caitlyn sneered as she and Amy walked by the car.

Cal slid down in his seat. He knew Caitlyn and Amy. Everybody did. They were two of the most popular girls at school. "Don't you know smoking gives you dragon breath?" Caitlyn said. "That's so gross. I didn't know you were a butthead, Brandon."

Each year 38 percent of all accidental fires are started by cigarettes.

More Than Just Dragon Breath

Having dragon breath and losing the respect of your peers is bad enough. However, as you probably already know, smoking can cause even worse troubles. It can lead to serious health problems such as heart and lung disease and cancer, to name a few.

Smoking not only can destroy a person's health but also can kill the person. In the United States alone, smoking-related diseases kill more than 400,000 people each year. These diseases are responsible for more deaths than AIDS, auto accidents, murders, fires, suicides, and drug overdoses combined. The last two causes of death refer to people who kill themselves and those who take too many drugs. Worldwide, smoking causes three million deaths. In the time it takes you to read this page, one more person will die because he or she smoked.

What Makes a Cigarette So Deadly?

Tobacco is the main ingredient in a cigarette. Tobacco leaves themselves contain hundreds of different chemicals. When tobacco is farmed, fertilizers and pesticides are added. In making cigarettes, even more chemicals are used. Therefore, what a smoker puffs is a bunch of chemicals. Many of them are toxic. One of them, nicotine, is addictive.

When a smoker inhales, he or she draws oxygen into the burning tip of the cigarette. The temperature reaches nearly 2,000 degrees. New compounds such as tar are made as the tobacco burns. The gas carbon monoxide also is made.

Tar collects in and damages the bronchi, or airways to the lungs. It can lead to cancer or emphysema and other respiratory diseases. In addition, tar can dull the senses of taste and smell, stain teeth and fingers, and cause bad breath.

Carbon monoxide is the same deadly gas that is in car exhaust. This gas cuts down on the amount of oxygen in the blood. This may contribute to the heart disease that is related with smoking.

Tobacco smoke contains 60 known or suspected carcinogens— substances that can cause cancer. A smoker inhales each of these deadly compounds into his or her lungs. On its way to the lungs, smoke passes around the smoker's teeth. It travels over the tongue, around the mouth, and down the throat. Once in the lungs, some of the substances from the smoke flow into the bloodstream. Blood travels everywhere in the body. Tobacco smoke affects many parts of a smoker's body.

Everyone who was anyone had come to Chantel's party. It was awesome. Even Jason, the varsity team quarterback, was there. Lauri watched him light up a cigarette. "Hey, can I have a drag?" Lauri asked Jason.

"Sure, go ahead," Jason said. Lauri took a drag off his cigarette.

"Hey, put that out!" Chantel told Lauri.

"Why? It's not hurting you."

"Where have you been?" Chantel said. "Don't you know you don't have to smoke a cigarette to be hurt by it? All you have to do is breathe someone else's smoke!"

Putting Others at Risk

Smokers are not the only people at risk from the hazards of smoking. People who breathe secondhand and sidestream smoke also are at risk. Secondhand smoke is what a smoker breathes out, or exhales. It contains all the toxins smokers ingest, or take in. However, the particles are smaller. That means they can reach sites deep in the lungs. There they can cause great harm.

Secondhand smoke is a killer. It is responsible for about **3,000** lung cancer deaths each year in the United States alone. In other countries with less strict smoking restrictions, the rate is even higher.

Sidestream smoke is dangerous, too. This is the smoke that comes from the burning tip of the cigarette. Sidestream smoke contains higher amounts of the chemicals known to cause cancer than mainstream smoke does.

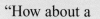

DEREK AND MIKE, AGES 17 AND 15

"How about a cigarette?" Derek asked Mike.

"No way. Smoking causes cancer. I'm staying away from cigarettes," Mike said.

"You want to try some chewing tobacco instead?" asked Derek.

Cigars and Smokeless Tobacco

You've heard about the bad effects of cigarette smoking. Did you also know that smoking cigars and using smokeless tobacco can be just as risky? The Centers for Disease Control and Prevention surveyed high school teens. Of these teens, 27 percent said they had smoked at least one cigar in the previous year. Cigar smoking may not get as much publicity as cigarette smoking. However, it can lead to cancers of the mouth, larynx (vocal cords), esophagus, and lung. These organs are all parts of the respiratory system. Cigar smoking also can lead to other diseases and to addiction.

Nicotine is as addictive as heroin or cocaine.

Smokeless tobacco is called different names. Some of them are dip, snuff, plug, or chew. These kinds of tobacco are held in the mouth. Like cigarettes, smokeless tobacco contains nicotine and other toxic chemicals. The nicotine in smokeless tobacco is absorbed through mouth tissue and the digestive system. Smokeless tobacco can deliver even more nicotine to the body than a cigarette does. That means smokeless tobacco can be just as addictive as cigarettes.

Like cigarettes, smokeless tobacco harms your health. The compounds in tobacco can cause mouth sores and discolored teeth. Oral tobacco also is a main cause of cancer of the mouth and tongue. The risk of mouth cancer, gum disease, or tooth loss increases 50 times for people who use smokeless tobacco.

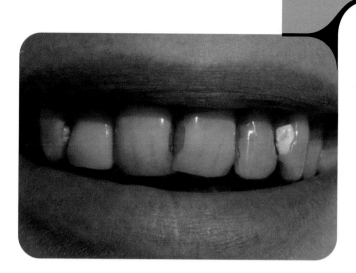

Points to Consider

Do you think smoking is cool? Why or why not?

If smoking causes so many health problems, why do you think people smoke?

Can smoking harm nonsmokers? How?

Do you think smokers who smoke in public places put others in danger? Why or why not?

What might you tell a person who uses smokeless tobacco about its risks?

Chapter Overview

Tobacco and smoking have a long history. It wasn't until the 1950s, however, that research began on the hazards of smoking tobacco.

Promotion and advertising done by tobacco companies has contributed significantly to the popularity of smoking.

Although people do get some pleasant effects from smoking, the health risks outweigh these effects.

Advertising, peer pressure, and curiosity are some of the factors that influence a teen's decision to smoke.

People who do not smoke during their teen years probably never will.

Chapter 2
Why Do People Smoke?

The Early History of Tobacco

American Indians grew tobacco long before Columbus landed in America in 1492. The natives of both North and South America smoked tobacco mostly for religious reasons. They believed tobacco had magical powers. To the Europeans, however, tobacco was a strange new plant. In fact, it was one of the things Columbus brought back to Queen Isabella of Spain, who had funded his journey.

Young white females are the fastest-growing group of smokers in the United States.

Curiosity may be the reason Europeans first used tobacco. Whatever the reason, tobacco use spread and increased. By the mid-1500s, tobacco was grown and used worldwide. It became a profitable crop, especially in Spain. By the early 1600s, tobacco was a major crop of the Virginia colony.

Until the 1880s, the most common way to smoke tobacco was in pipes. A new invention changed that. In 1884, James Bonsack invented the automated cigarette-rolling machine. Then, in 1892, Joshua Pusey made the first portable cardboard matchbook. This allowed smokers to light up easily whenever and wherever they wanted.

Tobacco in This Century

During World War I, many nonsmoking men became smokers. The United States Army gave each soldier a pack of cigarettes with his rations, or supplies. Tobacco companies started targeting women during the 1920s. They put ads in magazines that appealed to women. These ads worked. Women started buying and became hooked on cigarettes.

During World War II, tobacco companies again gave free cigarettes to soldiers. Also, cigarette ads played on radio and television. These ads tempted even more people to buy the product, and smoking increased. Around this same time, people were learning that smoking cigarettes was the most dangerous way to use tobacco. It wasn't until the 1950s, however, that research on the effects of smoking began in earnest.

In 1964, the surgeon general of the United States announced, "Smoking is a health hazard." In 1966, the following words were required on every package of cigarettes:

"CAUTION: CIGARETTE SMOKING MAY BE HAZARDOUS TO YOUR HEALTH."

In 1971, the wording changed to:

"WARNING: THE SURGEON GENERAL HAS DETERMINED THAT CIGARETTE SMOKING IS DANGEROUS TO YOUR HEALTH."

That same year, cigarette advertising was banned from radio and television.

Additional research was done during the following two decades. More links between health problems and tobacco were discovered. As a result, more people stepped forward to wage the war against tobacco and smoking.

Smoking Today

Today the evidence is clear. Smoking is hazardous to health. Smoking was once widely accepted. Now it is not. Today three out of four adults are nonsmokers. In the United States, smoking is banned in many homes and most businesses and public places. Even with all the evidence, however, old smokers continue to smoke and new smokers light that first cigarette. Unfortunately, most new smokers are teens.

"I remember exactly when I smoked my first cigarette. I was at camp and away from home for the first time. It was my first taste of independence. Lighting up that cigarette was just another way to say, 'You're grown up. You can do what you want to do.'"

ZOEY, AGE 17

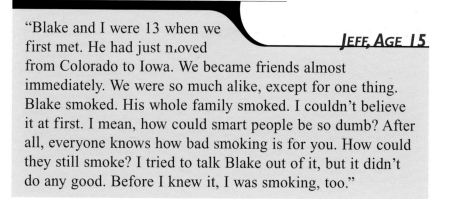

In the 1980s, Canada raised cigarette taxes to more than $3 a pack. Sales dropped almost 40 percent. Teen smoking was cut in half. In 1994, Canadian lawmakers reduced the cigarette tax. The rate of teen smoking rose again.

The Positive Side of Smoking

Some people smoke because of the positive effects they get from doing it. Some people hear that smoking will help them lose weight. The average weight loss, however, is only 5 pounds. People who smoke may feel that smoking perks them up, reduces anxiety, and helps them in social situations. Unfortunately, many smokers end up paying for these benefits with their health.

The Attraction of Teens to Smoking

To many teens the threat of ill health or death seems very far off. Most teens know the hazards of smoking. Often, however, a teen's need to rebel against authority or to feel independent is strong. Curiosity also is a big factor for some teens. They try smoking because they want to know what it's like.

JEFF, AGE 15

"Blake and I were 13 when we first met. He had just moved from Colorado to Iowa. We became friends almost immediately. We were so much alike, except for one thing. Blake smoked. His whole family smoked. I couldn't believe it at first. I mean, how could smart people be so dumb? After all, everyone knows how bad smoking is for you. How could they still smoke? I tried to talk Blake out of it, but it didn't do any good. Before I knew it, I was smoking, too."

Low self-esteem

A best friend who smokes

Feelings of rebellion

Depression

Being a poor student

Peer Pressure

Many teens start smoking because their friends do. Four out of five teens smoke their first cigarette with friends, brothers or sisters, or other teens. Only 11 percent try smoking alone. Role models also can influence teen smoking. For example, a parent, relative, or even a celebrity may smoke. If a teen respects that person, the teen may be more likely to start smoking.

Some teens feel pressured by their peers to smoke. They may not want to smoke but are teased or taunted into doing it. Other teens start smoking because they want to be accepted by a certain group. If they think that group is cool, they want to be cool as well. Smoking becomes their way of being cool.

"I hate to admit this, but I think the cigarette ads in fashion *ALEISHA, AGE 18* magazines influenced me. The women in those ads were my ideal. They were everything I wasn't. They were slim and pretty. They were having a good time. I don't know if the ads caused me to smoke my first cigarette. But I know this—they made cigarette smoking seem like a good thing. I know now that I was conned."

Advertising

Advertisements are another powerful draw for many teens. Tobacco companies spend billions of dollars on advertising each year. They are trying to sell cigarettes, but their ads promise something else. The ads promise fun, slimness, popularity, independence, and friends. These are all things teens want to have. However, cigarette smoking cannot buy these things. What it buys is something quite different. It buys teens an addiction that can ruin their health.

The Good News

Smoking is losing its cool. Both teens and adults are realizing that smoking is not worth the risk. Being cool and having friends and fun do not come from lighting up a cigarette. Here's some more good news. If you make it through your teen years without smoking, chances are excellent that you never will smoke.

Points to Consider

Why do you think Columbus brought tobacco leaves back to Spain?

Why do you think tobacco use spread through Europe and America?

Why do you think tobacco companies gave cigarettes to soldiers in World Wars I and II?

What do you think is the biggest influence on teens who start smoking?

Chapter
Overview

Tobacco contains a powerfully addictive drug called nicotine. This drug causes rapid heartbeat, narrowing of blood vessels, and an increase in stomach acid.

Smokers usually do not realize that they are becoming addicted to cigarettes.

Regular smokers go through withdrawal if they do not get nicotine. Withdrawal symptoms include nervousness and irritability.

Smoking is psychologically addictive. It becomes an important part of the smoker's routine and social life.

Smoking is a difficult addiction to beat, but it can be done.

Chapter **3**
Why It's Hard to Stop Smoking Once You Start

Nicotine, a Powerfully Addictive Drug

Cigarettes contain a powerful drug called nicotine. This poison found in tobacco leaves is the tobacco plant's weapon against insects. It kills them. Nicotine has a different effect in the human body. It does not kill the smoker because the poison is not absorbed all at once. The body breaks it down. What is left leaves the body through the urine.

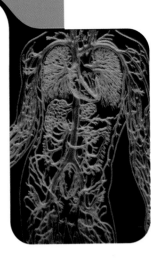

The body absorbs nicotine quickly. Once in the lungs, it is transferred to the bloodstream and travels throughout the body. It reaches the brain in fewer than 10 seconds. Nicotine makes the heart pump harder, and it narrows the blood vessels and increases stomach acid.

Nicotine can change the way a person feels, too. It can make a person feel either more alert or more relaxed. However, nicotine is addictive. That means a smoker gradually develops a craving or desire for nictone that is difficult to control. Because of this, cigarettes are highly addictive. That means smokers have an especially hard time giving up cigarettes. One-third of young people who try cigarettes end up being addicted by the time they are 20.

Addiction

Addiction usually sneaks up on a person. The process of becoming addicted usually takes about two or three years. That time period begins with a smoker's first cigarette and ends at the smoker's regular use of tobacco. During this time, the person thinks, "I can stop when I want." The person also may think, "I am not hooked." However, the smoker does not realize that nicotine has taken control.

Stages of smoking:

Presmoking—see others smoke, see advertisements

Trying—smoke first few cigarettes (usually with friends)

Experimenting—smoke on and off in the same setting

Regular use—smoke regularly in different settings

Addiction—smoke often and regularly because body needs nicotine

During the last 15 minutes of the movie, LaTasha could hardly concentrate. As soon as the credits started rolling, she grabbed Josh's hand. "Let's get out of here," she said. All LaTasha could think about was lighting up a cigarette.

LaTasha, Age 16

In the lobby, Josh spied a couple of friends. "Look, there's Rod and José! Let's see what they thought of the movie," Josh said.

"Forget it," LaTasha said. "I've got to get a smoke."

"Why don't you just quit smoking, LaTasha!" Josh said.

"Easy for you to say," LaTasha thought.

Withdrawal

A smoker's body is used to getting nicotine regularly. When the body doesn't get nicotine, it goes through withdrawal. The nicotine level in the body drops. When the level gets too low, smokers become tense and irritable. They need another fix quickly. The body needs the drug to ward off unpleasant sensations. Most smokers need about 10 cigarettes a day to keep from going through withdrawal.

Traits of addiction include:

Using the substance more than intended

Craving the substance and being unable to quit taking it

Feeling withdrawal symptoms and taking the substance
to avoid symptoms

Using the substance despite knowing its harm

The following is a list of some changes that nicotine withdrawal
can cause:

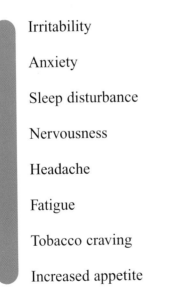

Irritability

Anxiety

Sleep disturbance

Nervousness

Headache

Fatigue

Tobacco craving

Increased appetite

Social Aspects of Addiction

Smoking is addictive. It also begins to serve social needs.
People get used to smoking at certain times or places or in
certain situations. Smoking becomes a ritual and a social thing.
This is another reason why smoking is so hard to give up.

Teens explain some of the ways they are psychologically addicted to smoking.

Kerry: "I smoke when I talk to friends on the phone. As soon as I think about calling my best friend, I want a cigarette."

Leah: "Mostly I smoke at parties where everyone else is smoking. It's fun and relaxing. Besides, it's something to do with my hands."

Phillipe: "After I eat, that's when I have to light up. It's my 'dessert.'"

Britta: "When I get mad, a cigarette calms me down."

Brian: "I don't smoke all that much except at coffeehouses. Almost everyone smokes at them. It's a social thing."

Smoking hooks both the body and mind. The body becomes dependent on the "fix" nicotine gives it. The mind keeps people smoking, too. Certain events and situations trigger a smoker's need and desire to smoke. These two reasons alone make smoking an extremely difficult addiction to conquer. However, it can be done.

Points to Consider

Ask someone you know who smokes how he or she feels while smoking. How does that person feel after he or she has smoked?

What does addiction mean to you?

Why do you think addiction is harmful?

Chapter Overview

Smoking costs both smokers and society a lot of money.

Smoking can affect a person's appearance and odor. It causes stained teeth, wrinkles, and bad breath.

Smokers are usually less physically fit than nonsmokers. They tend not to live as long as nonsmokers.

Smoking can cause a variety of diseases and disorders and may even lead to death.

Chapter 4

The Price of Smoking

Smoking is expensive. In the United States, the price of a pack of cigarettes is about $2.50. That adds up to about $900 a year to support someone who smokes one pack a day. In Canada, the price is even higher. A pack there costs about $4. A pack a day for one year adds up to $1,460. That's a lot of money to burn.

The diseases caused by smoking cost society a lot of money, too. The price tag of smoking-related health costs in the United States alone is estimated at $70 billion. The price of smoking does not stop there. More than just dollars go up in smoke.

Smoking reduces the level of many vitamins in the body. One vitamin of special importance is vitamin C. It boosts the body's immune system that helps fight disease.

"How was your date with Maria?" Kate asked Monte.

MONTE, AGE 17

"Okay, but her breath is awful. I mean, kissing her was like licking an ashtray. What a turnoff."

Physical Effects of Smoking

Smoking does not help people to smell or look their best. Smoker's breath is a turnoff to most people. Not only do smokers have bad breath but also their clothes smell like smoke. Most smokers do not realize they have an unpleasant odor. That is because over time they become used to the smell. However, an unpleasant odor is not the only cost of smoking. The tar in cigarettes can stain teeth and fingers.

Smoking also causes wrinkles. The blood flow to a person's skin is reduced if he or she smokes. Certain chemicals in smoke can damage the skin. Smokers are nearly five times more likely to get more wrinkles than nonsmokers. The wrinkles often are deeper as well.

Effects on Health

Smokers put themselves at risk for all sorts of health problems. These problems result from the toxic chemicals in cigarettes including carbon monoxide, tar, and nicotine. These are the three most deadly kinds of chemicals found in cigarettes. Of the three, carbon monoxide and tar are the most toxic. Nicotine is not the most toxic substance that is found in cigarettes. However, nicotine is important because it is addictive. Nicotine is the substance that keeps smokers lighting up. It ensures a steady stream of carbon monoxide and tar into the smoker's body.

Paco and David are twins. Both play football, but only

PACO AND DAVID, AGE 18

David smokes. He started at age 14. Today, both boys are seniors and play varsity football. Only Paco still starts for the team, however. David missed several practice sessions because of the flu. He gets more colds than Paco does. He also has coughing spells and shortness of breath. While Paco racks up the points as wide receiver, David warms the bench.

People who smoke are generally not as physically fit as nonsmokers. Because of lung damage, adult smokers usually cannot run as far or as fast as nonsmokers. Smokers also tend to get more respiratory infections than nonsmokers do.

Tobacco Use

Beginning in November 1998, Thailand was the first nation to have sex warnings printed on cigarette packages. The warning reads: "Smoking affects men's reproductive, urinary, and sexual functions. It deforms sperm and cuts down blood flow to the penis."

One of the major health problems of smoking is lung disease. Some types of lung disease are pneumonia, flu, bronchitis, and emphysema. In the United States, smoking causes nearly 85,000 deaths a year from these diseases.

Another serious smoking-related disease is cancer. Smoking accounts for about 30 percent of all cancer deaths. It is the cause of about 85 percent of all cases of lung cancer. This disease kills about 200,000 people in the United States each year.

Smoking also puts people at risk for heart disease and stroke. In fact, smoking is the most dangerous coronary, or heart-related, risk factor. It is directly responsible for at least 20 percent of all deaths from heart disease. That adds up to about 120,000 deaths each year.

People who smoke also are likely to have problems with their teeth, skin, and hair. They are at risk for infertility problems as well. This means they may not be able to have children. Male smokers are 50 percent more likely than male nonsmokers to become impotent, or unable to have sexual intercourse. All these tobacco-related health problems decrease a person's quality of life. At the same time, they increase a person's doctor and hospital bills.

In the United States, cigarette smoking is responsible for:

30 percent of all deaths from cancer

87 percent of deaths from lung cancer

21 percent of deaths from heart disease

18 percent of deaths from stroke

Death

While everyone dies eventually, nonsmokers live longer than smokers do. Smokers die an average of seven years sooner than nonsmokers do. Also, a smoker's quality of health is lessened along the way. People who smoke are likely to struggle with smoking-related diseases for years.

Imagine a ship as big as the *Titanic* sinking every day. Imagine more than 1,000 of its passengers drowning. That's how many people in the United States die each day from smoking-related diseases. It is a good idea to stay away from tobacco. Doing so can help you to look and feel better, live longer, and have more money.

Tobacco Use

Points to Consider

On average, a pack-a-day smoker spends about $900 a year on cigarettes. What would you buy if you had $900 to spend?

Smoking-related costs are in the billion-dollar range. What do you think some of these expenses are? Who do you think pays for them?

If you don't smoke, have you noticed how someone smells who does smoke? What was your reaction to the smell?

Chapter Overview

Tobacco companies use major advertising campaigns to get people to buy their cigarettes.

Children and teens were a primary target of tobacco ads. Hooking people on tobacco early meant years of potential profits.

Tobacco companies agreed to pay billions of dollars for health care costs of smokers.

Many tobacco ads show cool adults having fun. The hidden message is, "If you smoke, you also will be mature, cool, and fun."

You have a choice whether you want to smoke or not. Eighty-seven percent of children and teens say "no" to tobacco.

Chapter **5**

To Smoke or Not to Smoke?

ALISON, AGE 14

Alison stared at the cigarette billboard. She didn't quite know why, but it made her feel good. The model was slim and tan and pretty. She looked exactly how Alison wished she herself looked. Maybe there was hope for her. How wonderful it must feel to look so good. Alison pictured herself at the beach looking the same way. How great would that be? Maybe she would pick up a pack of those cigarettes just to try them.

Who's Selling What and Why?

Few people like someone else telling them what to do. Yet that is exactly what the tobacco industry has tried to accomplish. Tobacco companies have told people, especially teens, that they should buy tobacco products. The companies have done this through advertising in magazines and stores and on billboards.

Tobacco ads may not come out and say, "Buy our tobacco products." Tobacco companies would have a hard time coming up with good reasons for people to smoke or chew tobacco. So they have to try to get people to buy their products for other reasons. To do this, they focus ads on things people really want such as friends, adventures, and good times.

Tobacco Targets

Tobacco companies wanted to keep old smokers smoking, but they also needed to keep attracting new smokers. That is why tobacco companies targeted their ads toward certain groups. For years, children and teens ranked very high on the list. There was moneymaking potential in getting people to start smoking at a young age. Teens who were hooked on tobacco probably would be buying cigarettes for the rest of their life.

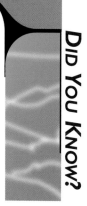
Unfortunately, the ads did their job. Two surveys showed that teens cited advertising as their number one reason for choosing a brand of cigarettes. Eighty-six percent of young smokers bought the three most heavily advertised brands.

Tobacco Runs Into Trouble

For decades, the tobacco industry manufactured and promoted products without being held responsible for the health risks it created. However, a lawsuit filed in 1991 began a change in the tobacco industry's luck. Janet C. Mangini, a family law attorney, challenged the tobacco industry for targeting its advertising to minors. The case went through many appeals. A trial date finally was set for December 1997.

Before trial, the tobacco company named in the lawsuit asked to settle the case out of court. An agreement was made. The company withdrew the cartoon character that promoted its cigarettes and replaced it with a different ad campaign. The settlement also included the company's release of confidential files to the public. Some of these files discussed youth marketing and the cartoon character campaign. They revealed that ads can and do get kids to smoke cigarettes.

In 1995, 134 lawsuits were filed against R. J. Reynolds, a cigarette manufacturer. In 1998, the number of cases filed increased to 664.

Tobacco Trouble Continues

Four states also succeeded in getting the tobacco industry to yield. Mississippi, Florida, Texas, and Minnesota all filed suit against the industry. Their cases claimed that tobacco product manufacturers were responsible for the health care costs of smokers. They also claimed the tobacco industry hid research and intentionally targeted kids. The states' final claim was that the industry manipulated, or purposely altered, nicotine to keep people hooked. The state cases were settled out of court. The agreed amount awarded to each state ranged from $3.36 billion to $15.32 billion.

Money was not the only area of concern, however. States also received agreements from the tobacco industry. These included bans or limits on billboard advertising and bans on giving or selling nontobacco merchandise such as caps or jackets. Also included were restrictions on the industry's ability to challenge laws regarding kids and smoking. The industry also agreed to release confidential papers. Some states received extra money to fund programs to reduce the use of tobacco by children and teens.

The tobacco industry faced lawsuits from 40 states. Instead of fighting each suit, the tobacco industry agreed to a national settlement in November 1998. As a result, the industry agreed to pay $206 billion to 46 states during the next 25 years. This money is for the health care costs of smokers. The industry agreed to spend another $1.7 billion for antismoking public-service ads. It also agreed to stop marketing to children and teens.

Tobacco Trouble Again

Several months after the national settlement, the tobacco industry was in court again. This time the case was a class-action lawsuit. That means not just one person but thousands of smokers with illnesses were involved.

The jury in this case found the tobacco companies liable, or responsible. The amount of money awarded for damages might exceed that of the national settlement. However, this case may be thrown out of court for technical reasons. The importance of this case, however, is the message from the jury: The tobacco industry is liable.

The jury agreed with smokers on several issues:

The tobacco industry deceived smokers about the dangers of smoking.

The industry hid tobacco research results.

The industry stopped scientific work that promised to produce safer cigarettes.

The tobacco industry advertised to children and teens.

Canada Fights Back

Canada also is waging war against tobacco. The government passed the Federal Tobacco Act on April 25, 1999. The Tobacco Act has four main goals:

Restrict access of cigarettes to people younger than 18.

Protect children and teens from encouragement to smoke.

Protect Canadians from diseases caused by tobacco.

Increase public awareness of the dangers tobacco products pose to health.

The act allows government to place limits on cigarette and tobacco promotion. It also lets government set standards for packaging, labeling, sales, and distribution. The government also can set a maximum allowable level of nicotine, tar, and other toxic substances in the manufacturing of cigarettes.

Provinces also are getting involved. In June 1997, British Columbia's government passed the Tobacco Damages Recovery Act. This act allows government and individuals to take the tobacco industry to court.

Make Your Own Decision

Advertising helps promote and reinforce, or strengthen, a smoker's addiction. Tobacco ads make smoking look cool. Ads show smokers as ideal adults. People look happy. They work and play with enthusiasm. They seem to be risk takers who enjoy the present moment. All these qualities are appealing. The message of these ads is: If you smoke you will be cool, mature, and exciting.

Cigarette ads try to get you to think smoking will buy you these qualities. Why? To sell cigarettes, of course. The more cigarettes people buy, the richer the tobacco companies become. The question is whether they can deliver on their promises. Will smoking really buy you independence, friends, and fun? Are the tobacco companies selling you the truth or a smoke screen?

The tobacco companies want you to start smoking or to keep on smoking. They need you to replace smokers who have quit or died. The bad news is about 6,000 children and teens try a cigarette each day. Of these, 3,000 will become smokers. The good news is that most children and teens are smart enough not to light up that first cigarette. Eighty-seven percent choose not to smoke.

ANTONIO, AGE 16

Matt pulled a pack of cigarettes from his pocket. He offered one to Antonio. Antonio paused but then took it. Matt lit up and took a long drag. Antonio thought Matt looked cool. Then Antonio thought, "No, Matt is trying to look cool." He wore horn-rimmed sunglasses, a white T-shirt, and jacket. Matt looked like a magazine ad for cigarettes. Matt had been suckered into an image. Part of that image was smoking.

Antonio stared at his own cigarette. Coffin nails, that's what his girlfriend called cigarettes. Antonio knew the risks. So why did he want to light up? Or did he? A picture in a magazine, is that what had hooked Matt? Did Antonio want to be hooked, too?

"In health class, our teacher brought in a bunch of cigarette ads. She asked us to think about what they were telling us. It made us think. Now when I look at any ad, I ask myself, 'What are they selling? If I buy their product, will I really get it?' The answer is usually 'no.'"—Greg, age 16

Points to Consider

Many ads focus on the product they are selling. Why don't cigarette ads focus on cigarettes?

Many cigarette ads show attractive people having a good time. Do you think these ads make teens want to buy cigarettes? Why or why not?

Do you think the national tobacco settlement was fair? Why or why not?

Do advertisements affect your decision to smoke or not to smoke? Why or why not?

Chapter Overview

Most people who start smoking want to quit. A person must want to quit smoking to succeed in stopping.

Having a plan to quit smoking is essential for success. It is a good idea to get as much information as possible before developing a plan.

Controlling the urge to smoke is the difficult part of quitting.

Aids such as nicotine gum and the nicotine patch may help smokers to quit.

People who have outside support have the best record for quitting.

Chapter **6**

Quitting

Sal sat in the nurse's office. It
was the third time this season
the coach had sent him. Sal opened his mouth to speak to the
nurse but started coughing instead.

SAL, AGE 15

Mrs. Gill didn't say anything. She didn't have to. Her eyes
said it all. Sal knew she was thinking, "You need to quit
smoking."

Sal was a talented basketball player. He had all the makings
of a future college player. Unless he stopped smoking,
however, his future in basketball was doomed. Smoking keeps
athletes like Sal from performing their best. It keeps them
from going anywhere in their sport.

Wanting to Quit

Smoking is an addiction that affects a person's body and behavior. Trying to change this behavior is hard. However, it is possible. The first step toward quitting smoking is the desire to quit. Studies show that 80 percent of people who smoke want to quit.

KIM, AGE 17

"I started smoking when I was 13. Both my parents smoked. They flipped out when they found out I did. They thought it was a terrible thing to do. Both of them had tried to quit many times and had failed.

"I guess I started out of curiosity. I took some cigarettes from my parents' supply. The first couple of cigarettes made me feel sick. I suppose I should have listened to my body, but I didn't. I kept on trying. Soon cigarettes had a different effect. They relaxed me. Before I knew it, I was hooked like my parents.

"Now I wish I could quit. My boyfriend hates it. He tells me it makes my breath smell and that it causes cancer and other diseases. Of course, he doesn't need to tell me these things. He won't let me smoke around him. He doesn't want to die young.

"I never should have started. More than anything, I wish I could quit."

Tobacco Use

Reasons for Quitting

Most people who smoke want to quit. This is because the reasons not to smoke outweigh the reasons to smoke. Some reasons for quitting might include:

You don't want to get lung cancer or emphysema.

You don't want to get throat cancer or any other type of cancer caused by smoking.

You don't want to get heart disease or have a stroke.

You want to have fewer colds.

You hate the phlegm, or mucus, in your throat and that nagging cough.

You want to breathe easily enough to play sports.

You don't want to have bad breath or body odor.

You hate those stains on your teeth.

You don't want to get wrinkles at a young age.

You want nonsmokers to be comfortable around you.

You would rather buy something more fun and useful.

You want to know you look, smell, and feel your best.

Not cheating on the first day you quit smoking increases your chance of quitting permanently by tenfold. One study demonstrated this. Nearly half of the people in the study did not cheat during the first two weeks. These people were still not smoking after six months.

Preparing to Quit

Many people are afraid to quit smoking. This is normal. Smokers who want to quit are facing the unknown, which can be scary. That is why it is good to know ahead of time what problems you might face. It also is important to have a plan. If you are a smoker who wants to quit, here is a plan you might try.

Decide how you are going to quit. Will you go cold turkey, or stop all at once? Will you stop gradually by cutting down the number of cigarettes you smoke each day? Or will you use a withdrawal aid such as nicotine gum or a nicotine patch?

Get help from a school nurse or your doctor. A nurse or doctor can give you information about your options. Some of these include nicotine gum, the nicotine patch, and counseling. These options are discussed later in this chapter. Gather all the information you can. You can get brochures at your school, the library, or any medical clinic. You also can get information from any of the listings at the back of this book.

Decide when you are going to quit. Pick a date no more than three weeks away. Mark it on your calendar.

During week one, keep a record of each time you smoke. Rate your need for each smoke. Record a 1 for a strong craving. Write a 2 for a moderate craving. Mark a 3 for cigarettes you smoke only out of habit or boredom.

During week two, try smoking only the cigarettes that rate a 1. Don't think too much about it. Just try to put off smoking.

During week three:

1. Get rid of any ashtrays you use.

2. Throw away your supply of lighters and matches.

3. Clean your clothes to get rid of the tobacco smell.

4. Stock up on gum and low-calorie snack foods. Keep these items in handy places.

5. Give yourself some motivation. This might include:

Posting on your bedroom door a list of reasons for quitting

Hanging a photo of your boyfriend or girlfriend who wants you to quit or a nonsmoking celebrity whom you admire

Keeping a jar full of water and cigarette butts as a disgusting reminder

Keeping a jar in which you put the money you're not spending on cigarettes

6. Tell everyone you know which day you are quitting.

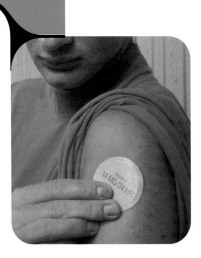

Quitting

The day you have marked on the calendar arrives. This is the day that you have told everyone you are quitting. You wake up this day a nonsmoker. You are going to do things differently today. You are going to change those behaviors that cause you to smoke.

One way of quitting is just going cold turkey. This means totally cutting off the nicotine supply. Another way to quit is to use a nicotine product such as the patch or gum. Studies show using a nicotine patch or gum doubles your chances of quitting. Each helps lessen the urge to smoke.

With the nicotine patch and gum, the nicotine passes through the skin. Nicotine gum must be chewed slowly. Then it is stored for a while between the gums and cheek. This is done to slow down the chewing, so the nicotine is not swallowed too quickly. Both the nicotine patch and gum are available over the counter and come in different doses. However, everyone should consult his or her doctor before using either nicotine gum or the patch.

Another method for quitting smoking is to quit gradually. That means the smoker reduces the number of cigarettes smoked over a period of time. One big problem with this method is that it may delay quitting altogether.

How to beat the urge to smoke:

"Find someone to support and encourage you."
—Renee, age 16

"When you feel that strong urge coming on, wait a minute. Take a few deep breaths. The urge will pass."
—Jalil, age 15

"When the urge strikes, do something! Take a walk, work out, go to the mall!"—Kaya, age 18

"Shoot a little breath spray into the back of your mouth. I know it sounds weird, but it works!"
—Janelle, age 14

"Stay away from smoking situations. This is hard at first if your friends smoke. But it's essential."—Hyun, age 17

"Keep your mouth busy. Cracking sunflower seeds worked for me."—Geoff, age 15

Whatever the method for quitting, it is best to have outside support as well. This can be a support group, a program to stop smoking, or counseling from a professional. The American Cancer Society provides a program. The address is listed in the back of this book. People who get outside help have the best record for quitting. The success rate for these people is between 25 and 35 percent.

Points to Consider

What do you think is the first thing someone who wants to quit smoking should do?

Where could you find information about how to quit smoking?

Is there something you have craved? Do you think it is possible for a person to control a craving? Why or why not?

Why do you think it is difficult for a smoker to control the urge to smoke?

Chapter Overview

You cannot make someone else fight an addiction.
However, you can help a person overcome an addiction
if he or she wants to.

There are five stages to quit smoking. Knowing the stages
can help you to help someone else stop smoking. It can help
you stop smoking, too.

To keep yourself from smoking, have a plan for how to deal
with temptation.

To keep others from smoking, be a role model or possibly
a nonsmoking advocate.

Chapter 7

What You Can Do

Trang got to know Liz in ninth grade. They were both in the same English class. Trang really admired Liz, except for one thing. Liz smoked. Trang wished she could get Liz to quit. She had no idea how to make that happen, though.

TRANG AND LIZ, AGE 15

Helping a Friend

Perhaps you know someone who smokes, and you want to help him or her quit. If that is the case, it is important to remember a couple of things. First, you can't make anyone else stop smoking. Second, there are five stages involved in quitting. The following are suggestions for helping a person at each stage.

"Today, lighting a cigarette in a restaurant is about as socially acceptable as wandering around spitting into people's salads."
—Humorist Dave Barry, *Kids Say Don't Smoke*

Stage One: Not Thinking About Quitting

At this stage, acknowledge how the person feels about smoking. Be a good listener. Help the person understand the effects of smoking. You could say, "Did you know smoking causes wrinkles?" However, you should not nag the person or say things like, "You're really stupid to smoke." The person will probably just get upset.

Stage Two: Thinking About Quitting

During this stage a smoker is thinking about stopping but is not committed to the idea. Again, be a good listener. You also can get your friend to think about what it is that keeps him or her smoking. You might talk about the benefits of not smoking. For example, if your friend is a runner you could say, "I bet you could run a four-minute mile if you stopped smoking." Present your friend with the facts about smoking. Do not nag or preach but be positive and supportive. You might say, "I know you can give up cigarettes if you want to. I'll do what I can to help."

Stage Three: Preparing to Quit

At this stage, the person is preparing to stop smoking. He or she has set the quit date and is open to a plan of action. During this stage, you can lead the person to resources such as your school nurse or helpful Internet sites. You also can suggest specific ideas on how to quit. Some of these are listed in this book. Others can be found through the resources listed at the back of this book. Remind your friend that quitting is hard work but is worth it. You can assure your friend that you will be there to support him or her.

Stage Four: Starting to Quit

This is the action stage. The person has stopped smoking. Get the person to talk about his or her feelings about stopping. Try to be a good listener. Praise your friend's success. Celebrate that first day and first week without a cigarette. Share your friend's success with others. For example, you could say, "Carrie has gone three days now without a cigarette. She's awesome."

Stage Five: Having Quit for Six Months or Longer

This is the stage when the person has stopped smoking for six months or more. Here is where you remind the person of the progress made. You can talk about the benefits by saying something like, "Your teeth look so white!" However, do not assume there won't be relapses. Help your friend not to be discouraged if he or she returns to smoking. You could remind your friend, "It's okay to take two steps forward and one step back. You quit smoking once. You can do it again."

Helping Yourself

"I smoked for three years before I even thought about quitting. **DOMINGO, AGE 19**
Then I started dating Ashley. She hated my smoker's breath, so I began to think, 'Maybe I should quit.' It took several more months before I actually made up my mind to quit. Then I had to decide how to do it. I chose to go cold turkey. It worked for a while. I lasted about three months. Then I relapsed. Now I'm going to try quitting again. And this time I'm going to use nicotine gum."

"If you smoke, believe that at some point you will be able to quit. Even if you've already tried several times, assume that someday you will quit."—Mara, age 16

If you smoke, it is important to be familiar with the stages mentioned earlier. If you are at stage one, think about how your life might improve if you quit smoking. This may help you move on to the next stage.

You can help yourself move from stage two to stage three by learning more about how quitting would help you. You could list the pros and cons of smoking versus not smoking. You may want to reread chapters 3 through 5 of this book for help on this.

If you are at stage three, tell people you are quitting and give them the date. Get help and advice from a professional. Gather all the information you can. Write down your plan.

Reward yourself for what you are achieving if you are at stage four. Remind yourself of the reasons you are quitting. Plan for what you will do if you relapse. Seek help and support.

Congratulate yourself if you have made it to stage five. Remember, however, change takes practice and time. Keep reminding yourself of the benefits of not smoking. Focus on your successes. Learn from your slipups. Often, it takes a few attempts before smokers quit for life. But you can do it, and it's worth it.

To Keep Yourself and Others From Starting

If you are tempted to smoke, you should ask yourself who will benefit from your smoking addiction. It also is a good idea to learn the facts. The more you know about smoking, the wiser the decision you will be able to make. Remember, a person who reaches 18 without smoking has an excellent chance of never starting.

What about pressure situations? How can you prepare for those? For example, what if you are asked to a party where you know there will be smoking? In this situation, it is a good idea to make up your mind in advance. Decide before the party that you are not going to smoke. Then when someone asks you, you will be ready with your answer.

RHEA, AGE 14

Rhea belongs to an after-school drama club. She wrote a play that makes fun of a supposedly cool character. In her play, the cool character does totally uncool things. The most uncool thing he does, of course, is smoke. Smoking gets him into trouble. It causes him lots of problems. The play is funny but has a serious message. Rhea and the drama club perform the play at elementary schools. The kids love it. The drama club hopes it will make kids think twice about starting to smoke.

Tobacco Use

"You can make things happen. We did at our school. The bathrooms were gross with cigarette smoke. The teachers just looked the other way, I guess. So a group of us plastered antismoking signs all over the girls' bathrooms. Finally those smokers got the message."
—Kari, age 15

"Have a tobacco prevention poster contest. We made antitobacco posters and put them in stores all over our city. People voted on the one they liked best."
—Reyes, age 13

How can you help keep others from smoking? Being a good role model is number one. If you say no to smoking, chances are your friends will, too. You may want to take being a good role model one step further and become a nonsmoking advocate. An advocate is someone who defends or maintains a cause. You could write a play like Rhea did. Perhaps you could compose surgeon general warnings like this student in Maine did: "Surgeon General's Warning—Smoking will cause social problems, health complications, and death. Quit now or forever hold your breath."

Points to Consider

You have a friend who smokes but is thinking about quitting. What could you do to help that friend to the next stage?

You have a friend who quit smoking but has started up again. What would you say to encourage this friend?

What are some things you can do to keep yourself from smoking?

What are some things you might do to discourage other people from smoking?

Glossary

bronchitis (brong-KYE-tiss)—redness and swelling of the membranes of the bronchial tubes, which go into the lungs

carbon monoxide (KAR-buhn muh-NOK-side)—a poisonous gas

coronary (KOR-uh-ner-ee)—relating to the heart

emphysema (em-fi-SEE-muh)—a lung disease that causes difficulty breathing

impotent (IM-puh-tent)—unable to engage in sexual intercourse

infertility (in-fur-TIL-uh-tee)—state of not being able to reproduce, or have children

pesticide (PESS-tuh-side)—a chemical used to kill pests such as insects and rodents

phlegm (FLEM)—mucus

psychological (sye-kuh-LOJ-uh-kuhl)—relating to the mind

reinforce (ree-in-FORSS)—to make stronger by adding extra support

relapse (REE-laps)—the act of falling back into a former condition or behavior

smoke screen (SMOKE SKREEN)—something designed to confuse or mislead

stroke (STROHK)—sudden lack of oxygen in part of the brain due to the blocking or breaking of a blood vessel in the brain

toxin (TOK-sin)—a poison

withdrawal (with-DRAW-uhl)—the period following the discontinued use of an addictive drug; withdrawal often is marked by uncomfortable physical and psychological symptoms.

For More Information

Haughton, Emma. *A Right to Smoke?* New York: Franklin Watts, 1997.

Hirschfelder, Arlene B. *Kick Butts: A Kid's Action Guide to a Tobacco-Free America.* Parsippany, NJ: Julian Messner, 1998.

Lang, Susan S., and Beth H. Marks. *Teens and Tobacco: A Fatal Attraction.* New York: Twenty-First Century Books, 1996.

McMillan, Daniel. *Teen Smoking: Understanding the Risks.* Springfield, NJ: Enslow Publishers, 1998.

Pringle, Laurence P. *Smoking: A Risky Business.* New York: William Morrow, 1996.

Useful Addresses and Internet Sites

Action on Smoking and Health (ASH)
2013 H Street Northwest
Washington, DC 20006

American Cancer Society
1599 Clifton Road Northeast
Atlanta, GA 30329
1-800-ACS-2345

The Canadian Lung Association
National Office
1900 City Park Drive, Suite 508
Gloucester, ON K1J 1A3
CANADA

Do It Now Foundation
Box 27568
Tempe, AZ 85285
www.doitnow.org

drkoop.com: Tackling Tobacco
go.drkoop.com/wellness/tobacco
Offers news about tobacco as well as a 24-hour
chat room to contact others who are trying to
stop their tobacco use

Health Canada: Tobacco Reduction
www.hc-sc.gc.ca/main/hppb/tobaccoreduction
Assists Canadians in working toward a goal of
a tobacco-free Canada

National Center for Tobacco-Free Kids
www.tobaccofreekids.org
Works to protect children and teens from
tobacco addiction and exposure to secondhand
smoke

University of Michigan Health Systems—
Adolescents and Young Adults
www.med.umich.edu/1libr/child/young00.htm
Provides information and links to sites
regarding smoking and smokeless tobacco and
their medical effects

Index

Index continued